Can you imagine...?

Can you imagine...?

a Counting book

Text and Graphics
by Beau Gardner

G. P. Putnam's Sons, New York

1 one

1 whale wearing a veil?

2 two

2 ducks driving trucks?

3 three

3 giraffes
taking photographs?

4   four

4 armadillos
sleeping on pillows?

5 five

5 bears climbing stairs?

6 six

6 goats trying on coats?

7 seven

7 raccoons carrying balloons

8 eight

8 snakes serving cakes?

9 nine

9 pigs wearing wigs?

10 ten

10 otters
playing on teeter-totters?

11 eleven

11 squirrels dressed in pearls?

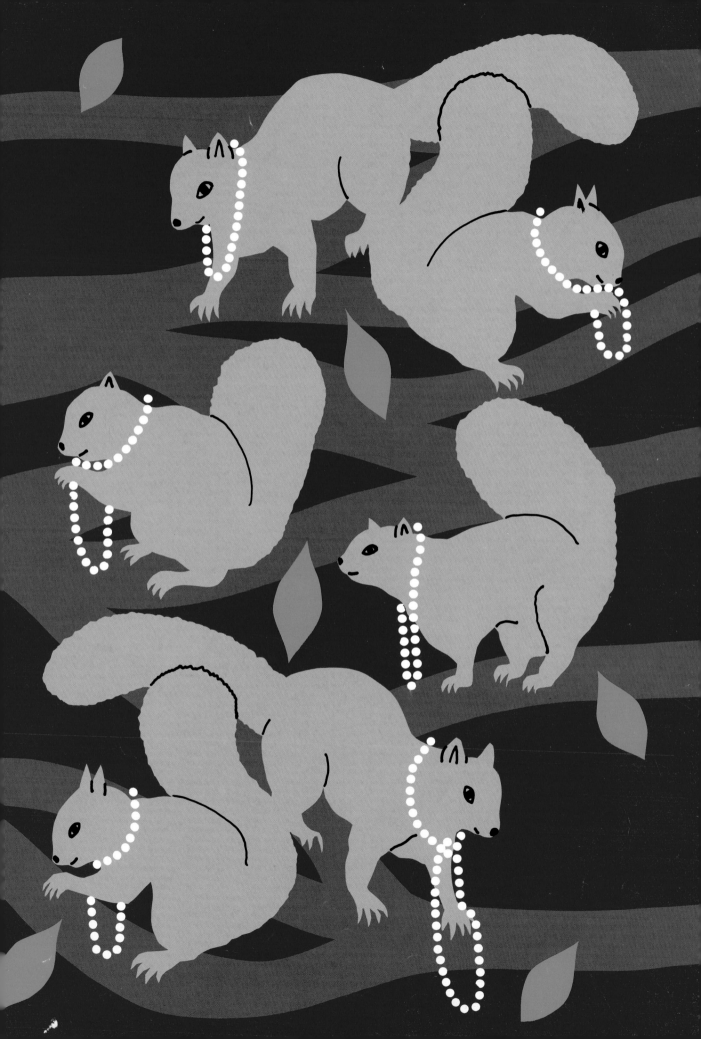

12 twelve

12 swans twirling batons?

1 one

2 two

3 three

4 four

5 five

6 six

7 seven

8 eight

9 nine

10 ten

11 eleven

12 twelve

To my
daughters,
nephews and
nieces:

Stacey
Mari
Keri
Kami
Steffani
John
Mark
Michael
Matt
Jeremy
Susanne
Glenn
Brian
Joey
Krissy
Tommy
Beau
Brandon
Jay
David

With special
thanks to:

Anne Simon
Margaret Pascocello
Randi Steinbach
Betty Schwartz

Originally published in 1987
by Dodd, Mead & Company, New York.
Published simultaneously in Canada.
Printed in Hong Kong by South China Printing Co. (1988) Ltd.
10 9 8 7 6 5 4 3 2

Library of Congress Cataloging–in–Publication Data

Gardner, Beau.
Can you imagine—?: a counting book/
text and graphics by Beau Gardner. p.   cm.

Summary: Rhyming text introduces animals
and numbers from one whale wearing a veil
to twelve swans twirling batons.
1. Counting—Juvenile literature. [1. Counting. 2. Animals.] I. Title.
[QA113.G37   1989] 513'.2—dc19
88-27322 CIP AC
ISBN 0-399-22027-5